The Invention of Wings

by

Sue Monk Kidd

A 30-MINUTE CHAPTER-BY-CHAPTER SUMMARY & REVIEW

List of Characters   4

Book Overview   8

Chapter Summaries   11

Part One | November 1803–February 1805   12

Part Two | February 1811–December 1812   20

Part Three | October 1818–November 1820   24

Part Four | September 1821–July 1822   28

Part Five | November 1826–November 1829   31

Part Six | July 1835–June 1838   34

Key Happenings   38

Author's Notes   44

A Reader's Perspective   47

List of Characters

Hetty "Handful" Grimké – The Invention of Wings is told from the viewpoints of two main characters covering the details of thirty-five years of their lives. These characters are Hetty "Handful" Grimké and Sarah Grimké. When the story begins, Handful is a ten-year-old female slave who worked as a yard girl for the well-to-do Grimké family living in Charleston, South Carolina in November 1803.

Sarah Grimké – The second main character of the story is Sarah Grimké. At the beginning of the book, she is the eleven-year-old daughter of the Grimké household. Sarah is given Handful as her own personal slave at the age of eleven. As an adult, Sarah becomes a well-known opponent of slavery and an abolitionist.

Charlotte (Mauma) – Charlotte is Handful's mother. She works as a seamstress for the Grimké family.

Mary Grimké (Missus-Mother-Mistress) – Mary is the wife of John Grimké and mother to Sarah and the other Grimké children. She runs the Grimké household with an iron hand and is a firm believer in discipline.

John Grimké (Master-Father) - John Grimké is Sarah's father and the head of the Grimké household. The Grimké family is one of the elite, wealthy families of Charleston society. John is an attorney and a judge in Charleston.

John Grimké – John is Sarah's brother and the oldest son of John Grimké Senior.

Thomas Grimké – Thomas is Sarah's brother and one of her closest friends when she is young. He teaches Sarah to read and helps to educate her.

Mary Grimké – Mary is Sarah's sister. She is named after her mother and seems to have inherited her mother's mean temperament. Like her mother, she is cruel to the slaves and does not tolerate any disobedience.

Frederick, Anna, Eliza, Ben, Henry, and Charles Grimké - Siblings of Sarah Grimké.

Angelina (Nina) Grimké – Nina is Sarah's youngest sister. Nina looks to Sarah as a mother figure. As adults, Nina and Sarah work together and become well-known abolitionists.

Aunt-Sister – Aunt-Sister is the slave who works as the cook for the Grimké household.

Tomfry – Tomfry is the slave who works as the butler at the Grimké household.

Mariah, Snow, Prince, Cindie, Binah, Rosetta, Eli, Lucy, Phoebe, and Sabe - Additional slaves in the Grimké household.

Burke Williams – Burke Williams pretends to be a suitor of Sarah but is found to be dishonorable.

Denmark Vesey – Denmark Vesey is a slave who won the East Bay Street lottery and used the money to buy his freedom and his own house as a free black man. Handful's mother, Charlotte, sneaks away to visit him whenever she can.

Goodis – Goodis is a slave who works as the footman for the Grimkés.

Israel Morris – Israel Morris is a Quaker man who lives in Philadelphia and who, after his wife dies, allows Sarah to rent a room in his house in exchange for her help with his children.

Catherine – Catherine is the sister of Israel Morris.

Lucretia Mott – Lucretia is a female minister in the Quaker church. She becomes friends with Sarah and allows her to live with her for a time.

Sky – Sky is Handful's half-sister and the daughter of Charlotte and Denmark Vesey.

Reverend William McDowell - Reverend McDowell is the minister of the Presbyterian church in Charleston.

Theodore Weld – Theodore Weld is an activist and abolitionist. He courts Nina Grimké and eventually marries her.

Book Overview

The Invention of Wings was written by Sue Monk Kidd and published by The Penguin Group, c2014. The book is 238 pages long and is written from the points of view of the two main characters, Handful Grimké and Sarah Grimké. The story is told in alternating narrative chapters from Handful and Sarah and spans over 35 years of their lives.

Sarah is the daughter of John and Mary Grimké, members of high society in Charleston, South Carolina. As the story begins, Sarah is eleven years old. Handful is the ten-year-old slave girl who is given to Sarah as a birthday present to be her personal slave. The two girls become uneasy friends whose lives are entwined over the next 35 years.

Sarah witnesses the whipping of a slave at a young age, and this upsets her so much that it causes her to have a stuttering problem. This affliction with her speech comes and goes at different times.

Sarah is against the practice of slavery and is horrified to be named the owner of Handful. She wants to give Handful back to her mother, but her mother refuses. She attempts to set Handful free, but this attempt is also thwarted.

Handful grows up and is witness to the torture, degradation, oppression, and horror that is afflicted on the slaves around her and on herself. She is whipped the first time as a child because Sarah taught her to read. Knowledge of reading was the one thing that Sarah thought she could give to Handful that would bring her closer to having freedom. Sarah is also punished. She is banned from her father's library and is allowed to learn about only the subjects considered proper for a young lady.

All her life, Sarah feels that she is destined for a greater purpose. Although society expects her to be a wife and mother, she rebels against it. At first she dreams of being a lawyer. She is ridiculed and blocked from this dream by her father and brothers. Later she seeks to be a female minister for the Quakers. As she is working toward this dream, Israel Morris asks her to marry him. He makes it clear, though, that if she becomes his wife, he will not approve of her also being a minister. Although she loves Israel, she turns down his proposal. At last Sarah realizes that her true purpose in life is to work as an abolitionist, writing pamphlets and giving speeches in support of abolishing slavery. She also becomes a proponent of women's rights.

Handful's mother is arrested by the City Guard when she refuses to move out of the way of a white woman. She escapes the guard, however, and runs away, disappearing into the city. Handful is saddened by the fact that her mother disappears. She becomes the seamstress of the household in her mother's place. She spends much time wondering what has happened to her and whether or not she is still alive. Eventually, her mother does return, but she dies not long after that. At the end of the book, Handful devises a plan to escape with her half-sister. Sarah does what she can to aid Handful with her plan.

Chapter Summaries

Part One | November 1803–February 1805

Hetty Handful Grimké

Hetty "Handful" Grimké is introduced as a slave yard girl who works for the John Grimké household. She is the daughter of Charlotte, seamstress for the household. The mistress of the Grimké household is a strict disciplinarian and is often cruel to the slaves she owns. Handful is then called into the house by the Mistress for an announcement that will change her life forever.

Sarah Grimké

Sarah Grimké is introduced as the daughter of John and Mary Grimké. It is her eleventh birthday and she is being promoted out of the nursery into her own bedroom. A flashback reveals that as a small child Sarah witnessed a slave being whipped. Seeing this event was so traumatic for Sarah that she developed a stuttering problem with her speech.

Handful

Sarah's mother ties purple ribbons around Handful's neck and then presents her as a birthday gift to Sarah to be her own personal handmaid. Sarah doesn't want to accept the slave stating she doesn't need a handmaid. Handful is so upset and scared that she ends up wetting herself in front of the party guests. Sarah's mother is upset by both Sarah's refusal of her birthday gift and Handful's accident.

Sarah

Sarah's mother forces Sarah to write notes of apology for her rudeness to all of the guests who attended her birthday party. Sarah gets the idea that, although her mother wouldn't let her return Handful, perhaps she can grant Handful her freedom. She sneaks down to her father's library to search his law books. She finds the correct wording to write a release to grant a slave freedom. She copies the words, fills in Handful's name, and signs her own name to the document. She then leaves the document on her father's desk. That night is the first time Sarah feels that she is destined for something important. She dreams of being a lawyer like her father. She cuts a silver button from her birthday dress and saves it as a way of marking the occasion. The button comes to represent this feeling she has about her destiny. When Sarah gets up in the morning, she finds the document torn in two on the floor in front of her bedroom door.

Handful

The first day Handful serves as Sarah's handmaid, Sarah asks her to build a fire in the fireplace. Handful does not know how to properly open the flue. Smoke quickly fills the room. Sarah opens a window to let out the smoke, which is seen from the yard below. Tomfry sees the smoke and starts yelling, "Fire, Fire." This gets the whole house in an uproar before Sarah can let everyone know what really happened. When Sarah's mother realizes what has happened, she strikes Handful on the back of her head with her cane. It is a vicious blow that knocks Handful

to her knees, but Handful is defiant and jumps right back on her feet
again.

Sarah

Sarah eats her meals in her room for three days to protest being given
Handful as a birthday gift. When she finally returns to the breakfast
table, her mother calls her attempt to free Handful a folly.

Handful

Handful makes several more mistakes as Sarah's handmaid that first
week. Sarah keeps it all secret in an attempt to protect Handful from her
mother. From a window in the hallway, Handful is able to see the water
in the harbor where it leads to the ocean. She has never been able to see
it before and loves to watch it.

Sarah

Sarah wakes up to find Handful gone from her post on the floor outside
her door. She goes into the yard to look for her. She finds Charlotte,
Handful's mother, and starts to talk to her. She feels compelled to
apologize to Charlotte for the fact that Handful is now her handmaid.
Charlotte tells her that she knows she will do right by Handful. Before
realizing it, Sarah finds herself promising to Charlotte that she will do
whatever she can to find a way to give Handful her freedom.

Handful

While Sarah is away with her mother and sisters, Handful snoops
through her belongings and steals a spool of red thread. Later, all the
slaves are gathered together in the dining room because things have gone
missing. Mistress Grimké is very upset with them because her bolt of
green silk cloth is missing. She is trying to find out who stole it. The
slaves are afraid someone will be sent to the Work House to be punished.
The missing cloth is found in Charlotte's room.

Sarah

On Easter Sunday, the Grimké family attends church. Sarah is to teach
the slave children their Sunday school lesson that day. Instead, she
teaches the children the alphabet song. This gets her in trouble with the
minister.

Handful

Charlotte's punishment for stealing will be the one-legged punishment.
While standing, one of her legs is tied up behind her to her neck with a
leather strap. If she lets the weight of her ankle drop, the strap will choke
her. Tomfry ties her up and then backs away. Charlotte immediately falls
hard to the ground, cutting open her head. The strap jerks back her head
and chokes her. Tomfry gets her back on her feet again. She is made to
stand like that for an hour. Charlotte survives the punishment, but she is
forever changed. She is filled with hate.

Sarah

Sarah is made to write an apology to the minister for teaching the slave children the alphabet song. She studies with her brother Thomas. Thomas confesses to her that he wants to be a minister but that their father will not allow it. He tells her that she should be the one who is studying to be a lawyer instead of him. However, it is not possible because she was not born a boy. Later that day, Sarah finds out how Charlotte was punished. She starts to take tea and medicines out to Charlotte. Her mother tries to stop her, but Sarah goes anyway in defiance of her mother's command.

Handful

Charlotte tells Handful stories from their past and from Africa. She teaches her about the spirit trees and about how the black triangles on her quilts represent the wings of blackbirds.

Handful thanks Sarah for her help, and Sarah apologizes for the way Charlotte has been treated. Their friendship is stronger as a result.

Sarah

Sarah and Handful spend more time together and grow closer. Sarah starts reading to Handful and soon Handful is trying to figure out what the words in the books are. Sarah decides that teaching Handful to read is one kind of freedom she can offer to her. Handful is a quick learner and soon knows all of her letters and many words. Sarah warns Handful not to let anyone know about her ability to read. When Handful has learned 100 words, the two girls climb to the roof to have a celebratory tea. They share their secrets and stories on the roof. Sarah tells about her silver button and her desire to be a lawyer. Handful shares her stories about her mother's quilts and the meaning of the spirit trees.

Handful

Charlotte pretends to develop a limp, claiming it is the result of her one-legged punishment. The Mistress takes pity on her and moves her to a room in the house where she won't have to climb the stairs. Charlotte teaches Handful all she knows about sewing. Together they make a quilt for Handful to sleep on, made of red squares and black triangles.

A storm comes through and muddies up the yard. Handful takes a stick and writes in the mud, even signing her name. She is called into the house and quickly rubs over the letters with the toe of her shoe. Handful doesn't realize that the quick rub over is not enough, and the next day the letters show through, having been baked into the clay by the sun. Sarah's sister, Mary, tells the Mistress about the letters in the clay.

Sarah

Sarah is summoned to her father's library. He reprimands her for teaching Handful to read. He tells her that from then on she will not be allowed in his library, and she will be denied access to his books. He tells her that she will study only those subjects approved for young ladies. Sarah then discovers that Handful is also about to be punished with one lash from the whip. Sarah screams when Tomfry is about to lash the whip, but the punishment is still carried out.

Handful

Charlotte asks Handful to write her a pass signed with the Mistress's name so that she can travel about the town. Handful has reservations about doing it, but she knows her mother is set on having it. Charlotte starts sneaking out on her own once or twice a week. Handful asks her to stop. Instead, Charlotte plans a way for Handful to warn her if someone notices she is missing. Charlotte starts making money as a seamstress on the side without the Mistress' permission. One day Charlotte's absence is noticed, and Handful leaves her the predetermined signal. Tomfry sneaks Charlotte up to the rooftop. They concoct a story about Charlotte going there to look at the harbor. According to the made-up story, it was warm up there, and she fell asleep. Mistress uses her cane to hit Charlotte's head for being so foolish.

Sarah

Sarah's melancholy over losing access to books continues until, finally, a doctor is called in to see her. Gradually, she is able to put it behind her. A farewell party is thrown for Sarah's brother, Thomas, in honor of his leaving to pursue his studies to be a jurist. At the party Sarah jumps to her feet to make a tribute to her brother and proclaims that she hopes to follow in his footsteps. Sarah's father and brothers all laugh at such an idea, making it clear to her that it will never happen. Sarah is devastated. She tosses the silver button that represented her dream into the ashbin.

Mistress is expecting another child. As the time comes for the new baby to arrive, Sarah makes a special request of her mother. She asks to be named the new baby's godmother. At first her mother resists, but then she relents. Sarah wants to devote her time to the new baby since she has been denied her dream.

Handful

Handful rescues Sarah's silver button from the ashes. She decides to make a spirit tree for her-mother and herself like the one in her mother's stories. She winds the stolen red thread she has around the tree in the yard. Handful and Charlotte give their spirits to the tree so that they can live with the birds and learn to fly.

Part Two | February 1811–December 1812

Sarah

It's February 1811 and Sarah is busy attending parties, balls, teas, and so forth in the Charleston social scene. Nina and Handful are helping her get ready for a party. Nina, Sarah's youngest sister, looks to Sarah as a mother figure and even calls her, "Mother" which upsets Mistress Grimké. While at the dance party, Sarah accidentally runs into a male slave carrying a pitcher of punch. It spills everywhere, making a big mess. A young man, named Burke Williams, steps forward and takes the blame for the mishap even though he was not involved. Sarah and Burke start a conversation and step outside for some air. Burke asks if he can call on Sarah.

Handful

Charlotte begins making a story quilt that tells the story of her life through appliqued figures. Handful tells Charlotte about Sarah and Burke Williams, and Charlotte confesses that she is also seeing someone, a free black man who won the lottery. He used the money he won to buy his freedom and his own house. She also says that he is already married to someone else.

Charlotte makes a quilt for Mistress Grimké out of the fabrics from her children's clothes. Right after this Mistress decides to allow Charlotte to hire her work out to others. Charlotte saves the money she makes hoping to buy freedom for herself and for Handful. A new slave named Goodis comes to work as the footman. He has his heart set on Handful. Burke Williams comes to call on Sarah, and she falls in love with him.

Sarah
The Grimké family travels to Belmont for Thomas' upcoming wedding. Sarah misses Burke Williams while they are gone and writes him a letter, but she receives no letter in return.

Handful
Charlotte sends Handful into John Grimké's library to find out how much it would cost to buy freedom for the two of them. She finds out it would be $1,050.

Sarah
The Grimké family returns to Charleston a day early. Sarah catches Handful using her bathtub in her bedroom. She keeps it a secret.

Handful
Charlotte and Handful go to market, and Charlotte takes Handful to meet the man she has been seeing, Denmark Vesey.

Sarah

Nina tries a new massage therapy on Sarah's tongue thinking it will rid her of her speech problem. It doesn't help, but Sarah discovers that if she breathes and thinks of water she can speak with ease.

Burke Williams proposes to Sarah and she accepts.

Impeachment charges are brought up against Sarah's father, Judge John Grimké. His enemies charge him with being biased and overly righteous. The judge is acquitted but his reputation is sullied. He seems to age and become an old man overnight.

Handful
Handful finds out that her mother is pregnant.

Sarah
Sarah's brother, Thomas, informs her that Burke has proposed to two other women and that he is just using her in hopes of a sexual liaison. Thomas breaks off the engagement on her behalf and tells her she must withdraw from society for a time.

Handful
Hannah tries to cheer Sarah by returning to her the silver button that she had thrown into the ashes.

Sarah

While Sarah is in town, she sees Charlotte carried off by the City Guard because she won't step out of the path of a white woman.

Handful

Charlotte doesn't return home. Sarah tells Handful that Charlotte escaped from the City Guard, but no one knows where she is now.

Sarah

Handful grieves for her missing mother and all the sewing falls on her shoulders. Sarah returns to society. She decides to give her life to God and joins the Presbyterian Church. Because Sarah feels strongly that it is wrong to own another person and because a law prevents owners from easily freeing their slaves, she returns ownership of Handful to Mistress Grimké.

Handful

Handful finds the quilt squares for Charlotte's story quilt and sews them together. However, she can't find the money that Charlotte saved.

Part Three | October 1818–November 1820

Handful

Handful discovers the African Episcopal Methodist Church where Denmark Vesey is one of the minister's helpers. She requests a pass from Mistress so that she can go there three times a week. Handful plans to use the opportunity to visit Denmark Vesey to see if she can find out what happened to Charlotte.

Sarah

Nina refuses confirmation into her parents' church. Her mother brings the minister to the house to talk to both her and Sarah, blaming Sarah for leading Nina astray. Mistress believes that Sarah's influence has caused Nina to become an abolitionist, rebelling against the beliefs of the church.

Handful

Handful continues attending the African church. One Sunday the City Guard bursts into the church. They say the people there will be charged with disorderly conduct. They are all rounded up and taken to the Guard House. If their owners come to pay the fine, they will be released. Otherwise, they will be sent to the Work House for punishment. No one comes to pay Handful's fine.

Sarah

Handful's punishment at the Work House is to be on the treadmill. She falls off the treadmill, and her foot goes under the wheel and is mangled. Handful is returned home after her punishment. Sarah finds out that her mother refused to pay the fine for Handful.

John Grimké's health continues to fail. The doctor recommends sending him to Philadelphia for treatment, and it is decided that Sarah shall accompany him there. Sarah realizes that her mother is doing this to separate her from her sister Nina. Sarah doesn't want to go but has no choice.

Handful
Sarah comes to tell Handful that she is going to Philadelphia. Handful asks her to write a pass for her so she can go into town on her own. Sarah agrees. Handful uses the pass to go see Denmark, hoping to find out what happened to her mother.

Sarah
Sarah accompanies her father to Philadelphia for his treatments, but his health continues to fail. He dies and is buried there.

Handful
Handful sews the mourning dress for Mary Grimké. Handful seeks out Denmark, again trying to get more information about Charlotte. She

discovers that Denmark is organizing the slaves in hopes of a revolt. Handful learns that Denmark helped Charlotte get to another part of the city where she could hide, but while she was hiding, a slave poacher found her and took her away with him. Denmark does not know where she ended up after that.

Sarah

After her father's death, Sarah decides to stay on in Philadelphia. Later she returns to Charleston, and on the boat ride home she meets Israel Morris, a Quaker man. Sarah learns from Israel that the Quakers do not believe in slavery, and they allow females to be ministers as well as men.

Handful

The family and slaves are all gathered together for the reading of the Master's will. The house is left to son Henry, although the Mistress is to be permitted to live in it until her death. The will states that she can choose six of his slaves to keep. The rest are to be sent to the homes of their children or sold. Handful is one of the slaves that Mistress keeps.

Sarah

Sarah studies more about the Quaker faith. She writes a letter to Israel seeking his counsel. He writes back that his wife has died. He encourages her to continue in her faith and to stay in touch with him.

Sarah thinks she hears a voice (perhaps from God?) telling her to go north.

Part Four | September 1821–July 1822

Sarah

Israel Morris invites Sarah to come and room in his house. His sister Catherine lives there, too. Sarah is to help tutor his children.

Handful

Handful makes a quilt for Denmark with a special pocket in it to hide a list he has with the names of slaves who are willing to help in the revolt. Nina creates the Female Prayer Society where young women her age meet. She lectures them on why slavery should be abolished. As an example, she asks Handful to show the women her crippled foot, which makes one of the women faint. Both Nina and Handful are punished, and Nina is not allowed to continue with the meetings.

Sarah

Sarah and Catherine make a picnic to celebrate the birthday of Israel's daughter, Becky. Sarah asks Israel to take time from his work to join them. Catherine catches Sarah and Israel holding hands and says it is improper for Sarah to continue living with them. She brings the matter up before the church during a meeting, asking for help in relocating her. Israel doesn't stand up for Sarah, but a female minister, Lucretia Mott, does. The Quakers decide that Sarah must leave Israel's house. Lucretia Moss invites Sarah to come and live with her and her husband.

Handful

Handful listens in while Denmark is speaking to his lieutenants about the revolt they are planning. They need to steal a bullet mold from the City Arsenal, and Handful volunteers to do this.

Sarah

Sarah receives a letter from Nina requesting her to come home to help her, and this makes Sarah decides to return to Charleston.

Handful

Handful asks Nina for a pass to go to town to buy molasses for the Mistress. Nina knows it is an excuse for something else, but she writes her the pass anyway. Handful uses the pass to go to the City Arsenal to steal two bullet molds.

Sarah

Sarah returns to Charleston and hears rumors about a slave uprising. She asks Handful about it but gets no answers from her. Sarah and Nina set out to walk to a service at the Quaker Church. On the way there, one of the City Guards asks Sarah if she is a Quaker. The Quakers do not believe in slavery. The City Guard claims that Sarah, who is dressed as a Quaker, represents the abolitionists he is fighting against. He thinks she may be helping the slaves revolt, and he threatens to arrest her, but he decides to let her go because of who her father was. The City Guard begins arresting those known to be involved in the planned revolt.

Handful

Handful goes into the city to see if she can find out what has happened to the slaves involved in planning the revolt. She finds Denmark packing, ready to flee because he knows the guard is looking for him. Denmark is caught four days later. He is tried and sentenced to die. Handful slips away from home so that she can be there when he is hung. She doesn't want him to die alone.

Part Five | November 1826–November 1829

Handful

Charlotte returns home with her daughter Sky, Denmark's child. She has aged a lot. Her back is covered with whip scars, and her shoulder has been branded with a hot iron. Her two front teeth have been knocked out.

Sarah

Sarah goes back north and rents a room from Lucretia Mott. Israel visits her there twice a month and teaches her about the Quaker Church. As she learns more about the Quaker faith, Sarah feels inspired to become a Quaker minister.

She gets a letter from Handful telling her that Charlotte has come home.

Handful

Handful overhears the Mistress planning to sell Sky in the spring. Handful knows they have to find something Sky is skilled at doing so Mistress will want to keep her around. Handful puts her to work in the yard. Sky is very talented at gardening and makes the garden thrive. Mistress decides to keep her.

Sarah

Some at the Quaker Church feel that Sarah is too outspoken about slavery at the church meetings. Sarah wears her button pinned to her dress, which draws a lot of attention. The button is the center of an altercation between her and another woman of the church. Sarah gets a letter from Nina, telling her that she is falling in love with Reverend McDowell at the Presbyterian Church. Israel comes and proposes marriage to Sarah. She asks him if she can marry him and still continue to pursue being a minister. He tells her that she will have plenty to do as his wife and as the caretaker of his children. His answer implies that she will have to choose between being his wife and being a minister. She turns down his proposal of marriage.

Handful

Charlotte continues to make squares for her story quilt, telling more about her life. While away, Charlotte was working at a rice farm. The Master there branded a "W" into her back. She and Sky ran away from there four times. Each time they were punished. The Master had forced himself sexually on Charlotte when she first arrived there. This time, Charlotte had decided to run again because she was afraid he would try the same thing with Sky.

Handful takes Sky with her to town to teach her how to behave there. She also shows her where Denmark lived and tells her all about her father. Back at home, Charlotte tells Handful that the money she had saved years before is sewed inside the quilt on the quilt frame.

Sarah

Sarah writes to Nina to tell her she turned down Israel's proposal. Nina writes back that she has decided not to marry the Reverend. She went before the elders of the church and asked them to free their slaves and denounce slavery. This didn't go over well with the elders or the Reverend. This made her decide she could not marry someone who is such a coward. Nina decides she will become a Quaker like Sarah. Sarah continues her work towards becoming a minister, but her speech problems return to make it much more difficult for her. Nina comes north to be with Sarah, and Catherine, who has moved out of Israel's house and into her own house, rents a room to them.

Part Six | July 1835–June 1838

Handful

Mary, the oldest daughter, becomes a widow and returns to the estate bringing nine slaves with her. The house is full to overflowing again.

Charlotte wraps herself in her story quilt and then sits by the spirit tree. She goes there to retrieve her spirit, and then she dies.

Sarah

Sarah and Nina decide to sit on the Negro pew at the Quaker Church, knowing full well it will cause trouble. They are asked to move by church officials, but they refuse. The two women do this for three weeks. Then the church elders show up at their door. Catherine has a copy of The Liberator, an anti-slavery newspaper. A letter written by Nina has been published on the front page of the paper. The sisters are told by the elders that they have to recant the letter or be expelled from the church. The women refuse to recant it.

Handful

Handful sends a letter to Sarah to let her know of Charlotte's death.

Sarah

Sarah and Nina are asked to leave Catherine's home. No one else wants to board them, either. Finally, the two slaves that the sisters had shared a bench with at church invite Sarah and Nina to stay with them. The sisters are harassed whenever they step outside, so they stay in the attic like hermits. They then decide to write pamphlets addressing the slavery issue, one to be sent to Southern ministers and one to be sent to Southern women. As a result of these pamphlets, the two women are invited to New York by the American Anti-Slavery Society to receive training and give speeches in a lecture circuit.

Handful

Mary sends Handful to town to buy scotch. While there, Handful sees smoke and hears a commotion. She goes to investigate and finds a man from the post office throwing bundles of pamphlets onto a bonfire. Handful sees Sarah's name on one of the pamphlets. She grabs it. A drunken white man demands she give the pamphlet back, but she refuses and keeps going. The man grabs her basket with the scotch in it. She lets him keep the basket and runs away with the pamphlet in her hand. Handful doesn't hurry home because she knows she will be in trouble for returning without the scotch or the money she was given to buy it. She finds a place to hide where she can read the pamphlet. When she returns home, Mary has her punished with ten lashes. The mayor comes to the house to tell the Mistress that Sarah and Nina are no longer welcome in Charleston because of the pamphlets.

Sarah

Sarah and Nina's lectures are very successful. At first, just women come to the meetings. Later, men attend as well. Theodore Weld, who trained the sisters, asks them to speak only to women, but they refuse. Weld wants their lectures to be only about abolishing slavery, not about women's rights, but Sarah and Nina say it is about human rights, including both women and slaves. Sarah writes a new pamphlet on the equality of the sexes. Nina and Theodore Weld are attracted to each other.

Handful

Mary discovers Charlotte's story quilt. Handful is afraid Mary will have it destroyed so she has Goodis hide it with the horse blankets. Handful makes the decision to run away with Sky.

Sarah

Nina and Theodore Weld get married. Nina invites Sarah to live with her and Theodore. Sarah gets a letter from Handful telling her that she and Sky are going to run away. She also hears from her mother, who wonders if she will ever get to see her again. Sarah decides to go back to Charleston to see if her mother will sell Handful and Sky back to her so she can set them free.

Handful

Handful starts watching the boats in the harbor from an upstairs window again. She has decided that will be the way she and Sky will escape. She steals the Mistress and Mary's funeral dresses and begins altering them to fit herself and Sky.

Sarah

Sarah returns to Charleston. She asks her mother about selling Handful and Sky to her. The Mistress refuses, but she promises that she will grant Handful and Sky their freedom in her will. That isn't good enough for Handful. She is determined that she and Sky will run away.

Handful

Handful and Sky dress in the altered funeral dresses and put white flour gum on their faces. They wear gloves and veils with the dresses so that they are completely covered. Sarah helps to sneak them out to the carriage where Goodis is waiting to drive them to the harbor. She tells the butler that they are friends of her mother's. The three make it to the harbor and board the ship. The guards on the ship leave Handful and Sky alone, thinking they are white women in mourning. The ship sails, and they are off to find their futures.

Key Happenings

1. At an early age, Sarah is traumatized by witnessing a slave being whipped. This causes her to develop a speech problem.
2. Sarah's mother gives Handful to Sarah as a birthday present on her eleventh birthday saying that Handful is to be Sarah's personal handmaid.
3. Sarah does not believe in the practice of slavery. For this reason, she attempts to refuse ownership of Handful. When this is rebuffed, she attempts to sign a release to grant Handful her freedom. This, too, is denied.
4. Handful tries to build a fire in the fireplace but does it wrong, causing Sarah's room to fill with smoke. Mistress Grimké is so angry about Handful's mistake that she strikes the back of her head with a cane.
5. Handful discovers the harbor and the ocean and learns about it from watching it.
6. Sarah promises Charlotte that she will find some way to set Handful free.
7. Charlotte steals a bolt of green cloth from the Mistress.
8. Sarah teaches some slave children the alphabet song at Sunday school, but it gets her in trouble with the minister, who tells her it is illegal to do that.

9. Charlotte receives the one-legged punishment for stealing the cloth. This punishment changes her spirit forever and fills her with hate.
10. Sarah tries to help Charlotte feel better in defiance of her mother's wishes.
11. The friendship between Handful and Sarah grows stronger. Sarah decides to teach Handful how to read, and Handful learns very quickly.
12. Handful learns to sew from Charlotte.
13. It is discovered that Sarah has taught Handful to read, and both girls are punished for it.
14. Charlotte starts sneaking away into town and finds seamstress work on her own. Charlotte does this extra work for money. She saves the money hoping to someday buy freedom for herself and Handful.
15. Sarah's plan to become a lawyer is laughed at by her father and brothers.
16. Sarah gives up her dream and requests to be the godmother of the new baby.
17. Handful and Charlotte make their own spirit tree in the yard.
18. Sarah enters society and meets a man named Burke Williams, whom she falls in love with.
19. Handful finds out how much it would cost to buy her freedom and feels like it will never happen.

20. Handful meets Denmark Vesey.

21. Burke proposes to Sarah, who accepts his offer.

22. Judge John Grimké faces impeachment but is acquitted.

23. Charlotte becomes pregnant by Denmark Vesey.

24. Sarah's engagement to Burke is broken off.

25. Charlotte is picked up by the City Guard but manages to escape them. She disappears.

26. Both Sarah and Handful find ways to get past their grief and move forward.

27. Handful plans to find out more about what happened to her mother.

28. Mistress thinks Sarah is a bad influence on Nina and wants the two separated.

29. Handful is arrested for disorderly conduct for attending service at the African Church. She is permanently injured from the resulting punishment at the Work House.

30. John Grimké's health is failing. It is decided that Sarah will accompany her father to Philadelphia in hopes his health will improve there.

31. Handful seeks out Denmark Vesey to see what he knows about her mother's whereabouts.

32. Sarah's father dies in Philadelphia.

33. Handful finds out from Denmark that the last thing he knows about Charlotte is that she was in the hands of a slave poacher.

34. On the boat ride back to Charleston, Sarah meets Israel Morris, a Quaker.

35. After the Master's death, Handful remains as a slave for the Mistress.

36. Sarah learns more about the Quaker faith and considers following it. She feels compelled to return to the North.

37. Sarah goes to live with Israel and his family until Catherine, Israel's sister, catches the two of them holding hands. She thinks Sarah should move out and brings it before the church. The church members agree that she must leave the household.

38. Nina continues speaking about and working for the abolishment of slavery.

39. Handful steals two bullet molds and gives them to Denmark to use for the slave revolt.

40. Sarah is temporarily detained by the guard in Charleston because she has become a Quaker.

41. The slave revolt is stopped before it starts. Denmark is arrested, tried, and hung.

42. Charlotte and her daughter Sky return home.

43. Sarah returns North in hopes of becoming a Quaker minister.

44. Sarah turns down Israel's proposal of marriage when he makes it clear she will have to choose between being married to him and becoming a Quaker minister.

45. Nina feels ostracized in the Presbyterian Church in Charleston and decides to move North with Sarah and become a Quaker.
46. Handful's mother, Charlotte, dies.
47. A letter Nina has written appears on the front page of a well-known anti-slavery newspaper.
48. The Quakers say that the sisters must recant the letter or face being expelled from the church. The sisters refuse to recant.
49. The sisters write and distribute anti-slavery pamphlets. The sisters' notoriety causes the American Anti-Slavery Society to ask them to undergo training with them and go on a lecture tour. The sisters agree to do this.
50. Handful steals one of the pamphlets that she finds in front of the post office, where Charleston officials are burning them in a bonfire.
51. When a white man confronts Handful and asks her to give him the pamphlet, she hands over the liquor she bought for Mary instead.
52. Mary has Handful whipped with ten lashes as punishment for returning without the scotch.
53. Handful decides she and Sky are going to run away.
54. Sarah returns to Charleston and requests to buy Handful and Sky from her mother, but her mother refuses.
55. Handful develops a plan to escape on a boat leaving the harbor.

56. Sarah does all that she can to help Handful and Sky escape. They all leave together on a boat sailing off to what the future will bring them.

Author's Notes

The author stumbled upon the names of Sarah and Angelina Grimké at the Brooklyn Museum. She discovered that the sisters were from Charleston, South Carolina, where she was currently living, and wondered why she had never heard of them before. She researched their lives and decided they were to be the subject of her next book. In spite of the notoriety that the two women had during their own lifetimes, they are relatively unknown by most people in current times. Sarah was one of the first women to champion women's rights and Angelina was the first woman to speak before a legislative body. The author felt their stories deserved to be told.

The two sisters rebelled against their upbringing as part of the Southern elite to crusade for the emancipation of slaves and for racial equality. These were radical ideas at the time. They were also among the first to do battle for women's rights. The author was especially drawn to Sarah and the struggles that she faced and conquered. She researched diaries, letters, speeches, and other biographical material to create this fictionalized account of the lives of these two women of history, including a significant amount of factual details.

The character of Handful is more fictionalized than Sarah's character. According to history, Sarah was given a slave named Hetty as her own handmaiden, and Sarah did teach her to read, for which they were both severely punished. However, Hetty died of an unspecified disease a short time after that. So the author created a life for Hetty and imagined the relationship between Sarah and Hetty for this book.

The author also created other fictional events with regard to Sarah's life. Although Sarah was a poor public speaker and did struggle to express herself verbally, there is no evidence that she had a stutter. Sarah's confrontation with a City Guard in the street is another fabrication by the author. Additionally, Sarah never boarded with either Lucretia Mott or Sarah Mapps when she lived in the north. For the sake of flow in the novel, the author took liberties with time in several instances. She also made some changes in the information regarding the pamphlets written by both Angelina and Sarah. The author also abridged and consolidated events in the public crusade by the two women.

Regarding what happened to the sisters after the events in the book, the sisters retired from public life after Angelina's wedding. They started more than one boarding school and taught the children of abolitionists. "American Slavery as It Is," the document they wrote, sold more copies than any other anti-slavery pamphlet until Uncle Tom's Cabin. Sarah continued to write the rest of her life.

There were other deviations from history in the book. The author used her own imagination to depict the other historical figures. The other members of Sarah and Angelina's family she portrayed as accurately as she could with the information that she had. The author toured the Grimké house to help her imagine the everyday lives of the family and their slaves. All of the slave characters were created from Kidd's imagination, with the exception of Denmark Vesey's lieutenants. Historians debate whether or not Vesey's planned revolt really existed. Charlotte's story quilt in the book was inspired by the real-life work of Harriet Powers, whose quilts are archived at the National Museum of American History in Washington, D.C.

A Reader's Perspective

"The Invention of Wings" written by Sue Monk Kidd and published by the Penguin Group, c2014, is the compelling, fictionalized account of the lives of sisters Sarah and Angelina Grimké, who grew up to become leaders of the abolitionist movement and the women's movement in their time. Their lives as daughters of a judge in the elite society of Charleston, South Carolina from 1803 to 1838 are intertwined with the life of Handful, the slave, who was given to Sarah as a birthday present for her eleventh birthday. The author uses symbolism to convey parallels between the lives of Sarah and Handful. Kidd alternates points of view between Sarah and Handful, weaving the narratives of their lives together to show their difficult friendship over 35 years.

Symbolism plays a big part in Kidd's work. Throughout the story, she uses the black triangles on the quilts made by Handful and her mother to represent the wings of blackbirds. These wings represent the freedom that Handful and her mother so desperately long for. They are determined to escape the torture that is a part of their daily lives. The title of the book, "Invention of Wings" alludes to the freedom birds have when they can fly away to any destination they wish. This continues the theme of freedom. An ornate silver button comes to represent the desire and dream of Sarah to be something more than just a wife and mother. She feels that she is destined for a higher purpose and the button comes to symbolize that hope for her. She seeks freedom for herself by fighting for equality for all women.

Both characters face many challenges throughout their lives. Sarah witnesses the whipping of a slave when she is four years old, and it upsets her so much that she begins to have speech problems. She develops a stutter that comes and goes throughout her lifetime. As a young girl, she loves books and longs for education of the type her brothers receive, but she is limited to learning about subjects that are deemed proper for young ladies. As an adult she continues to read and learn as much as she can. Her desire to become a lawyer is scoffed at by her father and brothers. Later, when she pursues a position as minister of a Quaker church, the man she loves proposes to her but makes it clear that he will not approve of her quest for the ministry. Although she is continually ridiculed and forced to give up her hopes of love and a family, she continues to work for women's rights and for the abolishment of slavery.

Handful suffers a crippling injury from a punishment she receives. She witnesses the suffering of other slaves and suffers herself from the "discipline" that is meted out to her. Her mother disappears for a time, and she must face many struggles by herself. Her longing for freedom eventually becomes her lone goal. Her talent as a seamstress becomes the key to her freedom.

Of the two characters, Handful is the most believable. The author uses colorful language to show her patterns of speech as she relates her stories about Africa and her people. Her point of view never wavers. She is a strong spirit and always knows her own mind. While it is easy to imagine Handful's character, Sarah, on the other hand, seems more one-dimensional. Although, the book relates the story of Sarah as an abolitionist, she seems wooden and not passionate enough to be an activist in much of the story. The motivations for her actions aren't always clear, and she seems manipulated by the author.

Kidd skillfully depicts the horrors that were experienced by American slaves at the hands of their owners. She also relates the powerful and moving story of Sarah and Nina Grimké and their devotion to the support of both women's rights and the abolishment of slavery. Kidd reveals the parallels between women's rights and slaves' rights, showing that both boil down to "human rights." The lives of the slaves and their owners intertwine in complicated ways. Their relationships with each other aren't always clear-cut. Kidd reveals how Sarah and Handful seem to be friends and almost like sisters at times, and yet there is always a gap between them that can't be bridged. The author shows us that, no matter how hard we try, we can never really walk in the shoes of another, but kindness and compassion can get us closer.

Thank you for purchasing this summary. We hope you enjoyed it. If so, please leave a review.

We are interested in talking to you to learn how we can improve! Please email instaread.summaries@gmail.com to take a quick survey. We will send you a $5 gift card from the store of your choice upon completion of the survey! -:)

33524229R00030

Made in the USA
Lexington, KY
28 June 2014